Seeing Spots

And Other Visions

Thelma Rowley

First Printing—2003

Copyright © 2003 by Thelma Rowley
All rights reserved
Printed in the United States of America
International Standard Book Number:
1-888081-66-X

Good News Ministries
220 Sleepy Creek Road
Macon, Georgia 31210
(478) 757-8071

This book or parts thereof may not be reproduced in any form without prior written permission of the publisher

Contents

Ball of Light..5
Bread Dough...6
The Amazing Plastic Bubble...........................8
The Hard Boiled Egg......................................9
The Plug..10
The Stagecoach..11
The Ring..12
Power Over the Enemy.................................12
Greyhounds...13
Shooting Ducks and Sitting Ducks................14
Awesome Jesus..16
Christ's Sponge..17
Eating the Word...17
The Sentence...18
Laughing Heart..18
Obedience...19
Gifts..19
Platform for Prayer......................................21
A Fading Leaf..22
Available Healing..23
"The Shmoo"...23
String Thing..25
Seeing Spots..26
Without A Vision...27
Money...28
Ship and Rudder..29
His Precious Blood......................................30
Two Globes...31
The Dot on the Line.....................................31
Mourning and Sorrow..................................32
Stone Heart...33
Unbelief..35
Yardstick...36
The Loons...37
The Hem of His Garment.............................38

This little book is for my friends and sisters in the Lord:
This book would not have been written without my good friend Kathie Walters - and my very patient husband who allows me to do what God tells me to do,

Blessings to my special prayer partners in New Hampshire and in Florida.

I was saved in 1969, and I knew nothing about the Bible, even though I had been in church all my life. I first heard the real gospel message through my local Avon lady, Lee Seltzer. God bless her.
So I embarked upon my Christian journey, very excited and very hungry. The Lord taught me through many picture visions, some comical and all very basic. Then He would show me relevant scriptures. So, here are some of those visions - I believe they will help you and confirm God's simple truths that make all the difference!

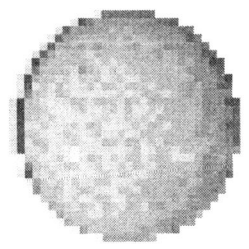

1. *The Ball of light.*

A ball of light came into my presence. The Lord spoke through it and said, "Healing is a choice. Choose to be healthy because it's My will for you to walk in My health and to receive healing." Jesus died on the cross for our salvation, our deliverance and our healing; physical and mental and emotional. He brings wholeness into our lives as we yield our members to Him. "Yield yourselves to God ....and your members as instruments of righteousness unto God" (Rom 6:13). "God is able to keep that which we have committed unto Him" (2 Tim 1:12). If you ask me to take care of your house while you go away for six months but don't give me the keys, then although I am willing, there is not much I can do to take care of your house. Commit your way to Him and He will care for that which you commit to Him.

In Matt. 4:23, Jesus "went about healing all" and in Mal. 4:2, there is "Healing in His wings". In Matt. 5:16, "... they were healed every one"; Ex. 15:16 states, "I am the Lord that healeth thee." "He was wounded for our transgression" (Isa. 53:56). "By His stripes you WERE HEALED" (1 Pet. 2:24). I can choose healing. Sometimes we see something in the Word, like healing or deliverance, but it seems to evade us. You know, God knows you and knows what makes you tick. He knows how you think, how you respond. If you put your trust in HIM and ask Him to show you how to receive, He will. He is faithful. His will is, that you eat from His table.

2. *Bread dough.*

I saw a vision of myself kneading bread dough, but it wouldn't form into a shape. The dough seemed as if it had a mind of its own. It would not conform to my hands. Suddenly my own hands disappeared, and hands like workman's hands came upon the bread dough. I knew they were the hands of God. Instantly the dough shaped into a loaf and put itself into a pan and into the oven. It went willingly when God touched it. "My people shall be willing in the day of My power." I asked the Lord what it meant and He said, "If you have one little pinky fingernail on the problem then I can't help you; remove yourself completely."

  When Moses led the children of Israel out of Egypt, he came to the Red Sea shore with the army behind him and sea in front of him. Feeling responsible for the children of Israel whom he had led out of Pharaoh's tyranny, he was stuck with NO WHERE to go. Then, God said something ridiculous in the natural, "Fear not and Stand still (he didn't have much choice) and see the salvation of God" (Ex 14:13). When Moses could do nothing, God came through with His mighty power and WOW!, a great miracle happened. There is no sea, nor army that can stand against the command of God. Most of us are "fixers" but we need to learn to take our hands off. When we call upon God to move on our behalf, we have to learn to stand still and let Him be God.

3. *The Amazing Plastic Bubble.*
    I found myself inside a huge, soft, clean, plastic bubble about 8 inches thick. I was at the top of a rocky, steep hill, and I knew the bubble was going to go down the hill. As it started to move, I was aware that I was weightless inside it. I was bouncing around inside the bubble. Although the bubble hit some huge rocks, I was not hurt, but instead, laughing inside the ball. There was no fear. I saw bullets and spears coming at the ball and I saw the indentations from the outside, but I knew I was out of reach. Nothing could puncture the ball. The Lord said, "You are always safe in My arms." Little did I know at the time that the devil would try to steal my life many times over.
    "The eternal God is thy refuge and underneath are the everlasting arms" (Deut 33:27). My friend once had an angel drive her car through a storm from Ocala, Florida to Orlando. While the angel was present

driving the car, she felt that nothing could touch them and no storm could put the car even the slightest bit out of control.

4. *The hard boiled egg.*

I saw a vision of a hard boiled egg with a jagged crack through the center. I saw Satan's fingernail trying to widen the crack to make an entrance. The movement was so subtle and even so gentle, that it was hardly noticeable. We need God's discernment. "Be aware and be on guard," the Lord said. Satan does not always announce himself, or make a lot of noise. Sometimes he is silent, like an undercover agent. The Devil seeks weak places. Make your weak point your strong point. "Be careful and vigilant because your adversary the devil, as a roaring lion, walks about seeking whom he may devour" (1 Pet 5:8). Sometimes something good can be the enemy of God, because we settle for a good thing instead of a God thing. The devil is tricky.

5. *The Plug.*

As I was meditating on the Holy Spirit one day (I had recently been filled with the Spirit), I saw a vision of a plug coming from a lamp. God suddenly picked up the plug and plugged it into the outlet - His Holy Spirit's power. The Angel spoke to Zerubbabel saying, "It's not by might, nor by power, but by My Spirit says the Lord." But even in knowing this scripture well, we still have an instinct to try to do something; to help God. But friend, it's His right hand and Holy arm that gets the victory. We must learn to put our own arm down. After all, it's the arm of the flesh and God does not get glory because of what we do, but what He does. "Stand still and see the salvation of God" is what God spoke to Moses. At the shore of Red sea, with Pharaoh's army bearing down on them and the big sea in front of them, we couldn't blame him if he shouted, "Run for your life, every man for himself." But he didn't. He was tuned in to God and he obeyed the voice of the Lord. When he could do nothing, he saw the arm of the

Lord move on his behalf and the sea parted right in front of his eyes. The next time you have a crisis - don't panic and run for your life, listen to God and stand still and believe. He will come through and get the glory!

6. *The Stagecoach*.

I saw a vision of a stagecoach, with myself and Jesus sitting in the front. I was driving the horses. The coach was careening all over the place, out of control. The horses were galloping furiously down a deeply rutted road. I was so frightened as I thought any minute we would be thrown off the coach. All at once the coach was proceeding with perfect smoothness and the Lord said, "Look who is driving the horses." I looked and Jesus had taken the reigns from my hands. I often prayed and confessed to the Lord that I was trusting Him for the salvation of my son, Steven, but when I didn't see anything happening immediately, I would try to fix things myself and I would keep pleading with the Lord instead of just trusting that He had heard my prayers.

7. The Ring.

The Lord had been teaching me about giving - in every area. Food, clothes, house, voice, cars, money etc. He had asked me if I would be willing to share everything. Then I had a vision of a coffee table in front of me. My wide, gold wedding ring was rolling back and forth across the table. My giving needs to be like a ring - continuously giving and receiving. "Give and it shall be given unto you"

8. Power over the enemy.

I saw a long hallway with little demons in front of me. The Lord said, "Use your authority against the devil." Then I began to rebuke them and take authority over them in the name in Jesus and through His shed blood. They suddenly noticed me and started to shake with fear. As they tried to run (they were very bow-legged) they clasped their heads with their hands. I was so amazed. After this vision I had great boldness. I began to invite people and groups of people to my house and teach them about Jesus. The Holy Spirit makes us God conscious, and that sets us free from being self conscious. We can, in Jesus Name, take authority over that which would challenge our identity in Christ. Luke 10:19 says, "I have given you authority over all the power of the enemy…"

9. Greyhounds.

I saw a dog race track with the greyhounds chasing the mechanical rabbit. As I watched the greyhounds the Lord said, "Never give up and never get discouraged." When the Greyhounds chase after their prey, they are totally focused. In the same manner, must we also chase after the One who is the Savior and Lover of our souls. "Do you not know that those who run in a race all run, but one receives the prize? Run in such a way that you may obtain it" (1 Cor 9:24, see also Heb 12:1-3).

Have you ever started to do something and then something else got your attention? You left the first thing and started to do the other thing. Then you noticed something else so you got sidetracked again. After a short while, there were all kinds of things going on. The result of the distraction was confusion and the first thing never did get finished. Often when we spend time with God, He speaks to us and instead of letting it "soak" into our spirit, we jump up to answer the phone. Or perhaps we suddenly think of something we should have done earlier, and we go to do it. Then that thing that God was trying to bless us with and deposit inside us gets swept away. It's one of the Devil's favorite ploys. Give yourself time; and then take time to do what He says. Don't let the enemy snatch away the seed God is putting in you.

10. *Shooting Ducks and Sitting Ducks.*

In a vision, Jesus and I were standing in front of a shooting booth at a carnival. A man came along and proceeded to shoot down the ducks on the belt running across in front of him. Then the Lord said to me, "Those ducks could be you without discernment. You can get shot down. Ask me for discernment." Heb 5:14 says,

"...those who by reason of use, have their senses exercised to discern both good and evil."

My friend, Kathie, was attending a meeting. Before the meeting actually began, people were milling around, drinking coffee and chatting in a side room. She overheard a man telling a small group of people how he had lost his wages on the way home from work (at that time people got paid in cash). Kathie felt a disturbance in her Spirit, but ignored it. She felt that the man was being dishonest, hoping for an offering. But in her natural mind she was unsure, so she ignored the prompting. The following week she found out that what the Holy Spirit was trying to tell her was right. The man had a reputation of going to churches and telling them this story. He did lose his money, but he lost it gambling in a betting shop! We have the discernment given by God, but we have to learn to listen to the Spirit. The anointing within you is to teach you the truth and also to reveal to you what is untrue. Jesus did not judge by the seeing of the eye, nor the hearing of ear; nor are we to judge this way. We have an unction, the witness of the Spirit within us.

11. *Awesome Jesus.*

I had an awesome vision of Jesus; I was standing behind Him with a large group of people. Jesus was wearing a great, heavy, gold crown and a purple, velvet cloak. The garment cascaded from His shoulders and formed a huge train. Brilliant large jewels encrusted the train. The whole garment was edged in long, thick, white fur. As I touched it, I saw the depth was from the tip of my fingers to my wrist.

Jesus spoke to me, "See My glory, My majesty and My promise of safety and security." Then He began to move in a gliding motion we all stepped upon His train. Suddenly I knew He was carrying us into the Holy of Holies. He spoke again, "The battle is mine."

Titus 3:5 tells us, "It's not by works of righteousness which we have done, but by His mercy He saved us..."

12. *Christ's Sponge*

I was meditating about Jesus one day, when suddenly the cross appeared. All the corners looked very square cut. Then I saw a giant sponge which had taken the exact form of the cross, almost as if it had been glued on. Jesus explained that He is like that sponge, absorbing all the sin and sickness of the world. We are redeemed from the curse; His sacrifice has made us free. In Isa. 53:4-6 it says that Christ bore our griefs, carried our sorrows, took our sin and healed us.

13. *Eating the Word.*

I saw a man's transparent body. I could see the cardiovascular system and I saw the blood running all through his body, supplying every inch. Jesus said, "If you will eat the Word, then it will nourish your body in the same way." The Word is our spirit's food. Just as in the natural we must eat to keep our bodies healthy and alive, so must our spirits eat of the Word of God to be healthy and to grow. The Scripture confirms this in Jer 15:16, "His words were found and I did eat them," and I Peter 2:2 "....desire the pure milk of the Word, that you may grow thereby."

14. *The Sentence*

I saw a vision of a written sentence. Three-fourths of the way through the sentence the hand of God came and put a slash line. He said to me, "You see the attention span of my people is so short and the discernment is so lacking that the devil is able to insert a lie at the end of a sentence and My people don't discern it, My people perish through lack of knowledge."

15. *Laughing Heart*

In the outline of a man, I saw a heart beating. All at once the man began to laugh. I saw the heart moving and the Lord said, "The laughter exercised his heart." I observed how much this improved his health. The oxygen increased in his blood stream and his blood pressure decreased. At that moment, I decided I would live in His love and joy. After this decision, His joy came into my life and I grew in health. "A Merry heart does good, like a medicine" (Prov 17:20) and "The Joy of the Lord is our strength" (Neh 8:10).

16. *Obedience.*

I was praying when I saw vision of a Bible laying open on the table. The wind began to turn the pages from Genesis to Revelation. As the last page turned and the back cover closed, the hand of God came and picked up the Bible, then threw it in the waste basket nearby. I felt so shocked but the Lord said, "You can know this book from Genesis to Revelation, but if there is no obedience, it might as well be in the waste basket." Ex 19:5 says, "Now indeed if you will obey my voice and keep my covenant then you shall be a special treasure to Me, above all people; for all the earth is mine." , ".....to obey is better than sacrifice" (1 Sam 15:22).

17. *Gifts.*

I had a vision of Jesus knocking at

the door. When I opened it, He was standing there with His arms full of beautifully wrapped gifts. I invited Him inside the house and he put the gifts on the coffee table. "I have all these gifts for you, all paid for. I paid the price," He told me. One gift in particular, was so beautifully wrapped, that it took my breath away. It was wrapped in gold leaf, the ribbon was gold lace and in the center of the bow there was an enormous sparkling diamond. This was merely the wrapping! He declared "This is my ultimate gift of eternal life." He then sat down on the floor and began to weep. I felt so hurt and crushed that He was weeping. Then Jesus said to me, "Most of my children don't even open my gifts." Gifts of health, well being, joy, prosperity, safety, righteousness, companionship, friendship etc., an endless stream of wonderful things that come from relationship with Him. At that moment I determined to take full advantage of every gift He had made available. I was determined to become greedy for the things of God. His

Presence and His presents. It changed my life, I never saw things the same again.

"......the gift of God is eternal life through Jesus Christ our Lord" states Romans 6:23. The Word also says in James 1:17, "Every good gift and every perfect gift comes down from the Father of lights...."

18. *Platform for Prayer.*

I was sitting in an auditorium waiting for a meeting to begin. As I looked up at the platform, I saw in a vision the platform divided into 3 parts. The first section was termite eaten wood, the middle section was made of cobwebs and the third section was made of sponge. I asked the Lord, "What on earth is that?" He replied, "That is America. She is standing on a false foundation and the only reason she exists is because of my mercy and grace." I saw the words MERCY AND GRACE written in large black letters. "That is what is keeping America afloat," I heard. He explained the vision further saying, "The sin of America is so great that she no longer stands on a firm foundation." Pray for the church to see God's purposes and intention.

"If My people, who are called by My Name, will humble themselves and pray and seek my face and turn from their wicked ways, then will I hear from heaven and will forgive their sin and will heal their land" (2 Chr. 7:14).

19. A *Fading Leaf*.

I saw a tree in winter time. Except for one little leaf, it was bare. Then a wind came and blew the leaf into the air and it dis-integrated. The Lord spoke to me and said, "This would be you, without Me." He is the life force within us. He also brought me the Scripture Isa. 64:6, "But we are all as an unclean thing and all our righteousness are as filthy rags; and we all do fade as a leaf; and our iniquities, like the wind, have taken us away." It's only God that gives life and sustenance.

20. *Available Healing.*

    This vision was a strange one. I was driving in my car and complaining about a pain in my back. Then in a vision, I saw numerous white strings hanging from the roof of my car. At the end of each string was what looked like a glob of white. The Lord said, "Healing is all around you -just reach out and take it." Isa. 53:5 says, ".....by His stripes you WERE HEALED." And Matt. 8:16 says that "Jesus healed ALL who were sick." "He sent His word, and healed them..." (Ps. 107:20).

21. *"The Shmoo."*

    I saw a line that looked like a clothes line. I knew it to be the line of eternity. I noticed "The Shmoo" sitting on the line. "The Shmoo" is a character in a comic strip called Li'l' Abner. "The Shmoo" has nothing except eyes and feet.

    I asked the Lord, "Oh, Lord, what on earth is this vision?" At that time I was having difficulty believing that God really loved me. He said, "If you never do another thing on this earth, never speak another word, never hear another thing, I will love you just as much as I do now. You cannot earn my love and you cannot qualify for my gift of eternal life." Even though He showed me that, I still struggled for a long time accepting His love. The religious spirit will try to make you feel you have to qualify or earn the gifts and love of God.

Rom. 5:1-2 reveals to us: "Therefore being justified by faith we have peace with God through our Lord Jesus Christ. By whom also we have access by faith into this grace wherein we stand and rejoice in the hope of the glory of God." Eph. 2:4-5 says, "But God, who is rich in mercy, for His great love wherewith He loved us, even when we were dead in sins, hath quickened us together with Christ, (by grace ye are saved;)" and in verses 8 and 9, "For by grace you have been saved, through faith, and that not of yourselves, it is the gift of God. Not of works; lest any man should boast."

22. *String Thing.*

I saw one white string hanging from the ceiling down into the center of the room. At the end of the string was tied a yellow tennis ball. I sensed the presence of the Holy Spirit. He began to gently blow on the ball and it began to sway very slightly. Then He went to the other side and gently blew it in the other direction. He spoke and said, "I want you to be so sensitive to the moving and prompting of my Spirit to the slightest degree - so that you will be sensitive to My voice and feel the slightest nudge and obey instantly." 1 Kings 19:11-14 says, "Go forth, and stand upon the mount before the LORD. And, behold, the LORD passed by, and a great and strong wind rent the mountains, and brake in pieces the rocks before the LORD; but the LORD was not in the wind: and after the wind an earthquake; but the LORD was not in the earthquake: And after the earthquake a fire; but the LORD was not in the fire: and after the fire a **still small voice**. And it was so, when Elijah heard it, that he wrapped his face in his mantle, and went out, and stood in the entering in of the cave. And, behold, there came a voice unto him, and said, What doest thou here, Elijah?"

23. Seeing Spots.

At the time of my salvation, I had very poor self esteem. I found it impossible to believe that God really did love ME. Then one day God showed me a small, dime-sized, bright sun-yellow spot right in the center of my chest. The Lord asked, "Can you believe I love you that much?" I felt I could receive that. Over time that spot grew and one day I noticed it was the size of an apple with the beginnings of rays like the sun throws out. I began to have a desire to serve people in the Lord so I started to taking gift baskets to the sick. Over the years, I have become more convinced that God truly does love me. The outward manifestation of it is that I try to minister to everyone I am able to. One of my most difficult struggles, has been the acceptance of the fact that God cared for me personally.

Rom. 5:5 says, "And hope maketh not ashamed; because the love of God is shed abroad in our hearts by the Holy Ghost which is given unto us."

Romans 8:39 says, "Nor height, nor depth, nor any other creature, shall be able to separate us from the love of God, which is in Christ Jesus our Lord."

1 John 4:9 says, "In this was manifested the love of God toward us, because that God sent his only begotten Son into the world, that we might live through him."

24. *Without A Vision.*

This vision was not like any other visions I saw. It disturbed me and gave me a burden for the Body of Christ; that we would know our destiny and calling. It was as if I were standing with Jesus and we were looking up at a curved hill. Tramping over the hill, was a group of people, somewhat like a rag-tag army. They had left or perhaps been displaced from their homeland. They carried various bits and pieces of luggage, some of it tied with string and rope. We watched as some fell by the wayside and did not get up. Nor did anyone try to help them. It was as if the others didn't notice; just continuing to walk despondently over the hill. Everything I was observing was in a yellowish brown color; there was no life in it. I felt very sad about everything I saw. I also was able to feel the sadness of Jesus for this group of people. Ephesians 1:18-19 says, "The eyes of your understanding being enlightened; that you may know what is the hope of His calling, and what the riches of the glory of His inheritance in the saints, and what is the exceeding greatness of His power to us-ward who believe, according to the working of His mighty power." Prov 29:18 says, "Where there is no vision, the people perish..."

25. Money.

In a vision, I saw old ship wrecks with their treasure buried in the sand at the bottom of the ocean. Then I saw money that had been buried on land, like an old tin can buried in the dirt with a wad of bills inside. Next I saw a huge bank vault full of gold bullion, stocks and bonds, notes etc. The Lord said to me, "I know where the lost money is and the found money, and it all is mine." He then showed me monies of the world; German Marks, Swedish Ore, Spanish Pesetas, British Pounds, French Francs and American Dollars. "The silver is mine, and the gold is mine, saith the Lord of Hosts" (Hag. 2:8), and Isa. 45:3, "I will give you the treasures of darkenss and hidden riches of secret places, that you may know that I, the Lord, who call you by your name, am the God of Israel."

26. *Ship and Rudder*

I was coming down the cement pier in Port-Au-Prince, Haiti approaching the liner headed back to New York city. Suddenly, I stopped and could see part of the rudder of the ship, still high in the water. I could view the heavy hawsers anchoring the ship to the pier. The Lord spoke and said to me, "See this ship? It has no need for the rudder because it is immobile." An expression people use is, "You cannot steer a stationary bus," in other words you have to be moving in order to be directed. Jesus, in the Gospels, declared "Follow me" nineteen times. In Matt 4:18-20, when Jesus told the disciples to leave their nets and follow him, He did not tell them where He was going. It was a faith thing. But when they were moving, they were in a position to be led. Ships that are not moving don't need a rudder.

27. His Precious Blood

When I was in Israel with a group of men and women, we were visiting the Garden Tomb. As I looked at the place where Jesus' body had lain, He spoke and said, "Go and tell the people." "What Lord?" I asked. I had no immediate reply, but the following day at the Kibbutz, where we were staying, the Lord drew me out to a small cactus garden. One bush held some red pods about 3" long. The Lord stated, "Take one and smash it on the walkway." I picked one of the pods from the ground and smashed it with my foot. A huge red stain appeared like a many pointed star. Jesus commanded, "Go and tell the people that I have shed My blood for them. Don't let Me have died in vain." His blood purchased our eternal salvation, security and deliverance from the power of the world and the enemy. 1 John 1:7 says, "... and the blood of Jesus Christ His Son cleanseth us from all sin."

28. *Two Globes.*

In a vision of two globes, I saw a man standing with one foot on each globe. The globes began to spin apart and a huge jagged crack appeared right up the middle of the man. Matt 6:24 tells us that it is not possible to serve two masters. Jesus said "Either he will hate one and love the other; or else he will hold to the one and despise the other. You can not serve God and mammon." Mammon speaks of money, but actually it can be anything that the world pulls you into. "Come out from among them and be ye separate" (2 Cor 6:14).

29. *The dot on the line.*

I was complaining to the Lord about some situation when He showed me a straight line with a dot in the center. Immediately I said to Him, "Oh good, you do see my problem (referring to the dot)." He instantly answered me, "Problem, what problem? That dot represents your whole life." I had to laugh to myself; He so quickly brings perspective into our lives.

 Temporary things can affect us so considerably, but in the light of eternity, they are but a vapor. Remember the next time you have a "situation" that these things come to <u>pass</u>. 2 Cor. 4:17 says, "For our light affliction, which is but for moment, is working for us a far more exceeding and eternal weight of glory. While we do not look at the things which are seen, but at the things which are not seen. For the things which are seen are temporary but the things which are not seen are eternal."

30. *Mourning and Sorrow.*

 I saw a vision of a woman standing with a line drawn across her waist. I asked the Lord, "What is that?" He said, "This woman has just lost a loved one and I will allow you to mourn for a season and to a certain depth of your being, but if you go longer and deeper, than my perfect will, it will eventually bring illness and a martyr spirit." A lady I knew lost a son shortly after birth. Of course it as very sad and she mourned the death of this child. But, every year throughout her whole life, into her nineties, she mourned and grieved. She never let it go and consequently a spirit of grief and heaviness stayed upon her and affected every aspect of her life. She had no joy and never laughed. Isa. 14:3 says, "And it shall come to pass in the day that the LORD shall give thee rest from thy sorrow, and from thy fear...." Ps 30:5, " ..... weeping may endure for a night, but joy cometh in the morning."

31. *Stone Heart.*

I had been praying, asking the Lord to help me be kind and loving. I felt as if I was hard-hearted and not capable of loving people as God wanted me to. The Lord gave me a vision of myself and I saw the Lord's hand reach into my heart. As His hand withdrew I noticed He was holding a grey stone heart in His hand. Then His hand reached back in and replaced it with a red beating heart. He gives us a new heart and renews our spirit. So often we think He is going to somehow improve the old man; but He came to crucify the old man (see Romans 6) and put His Spirit within us.

My friend, Kathie, told me one time when she was in a meeting, the Lord spoke to her to go across the room and love and hug a lady who was sitting there. "I don't know her, how can I go and put my arms around her and love her?" Kathie asked. "The love of God IS shed abroad in your heart by the Holy Ghost," the Lord replied. (Rom 5:5) By faith, Kathie went over and put her arms around the lady. As she did, the love of God swept through her and touched this precious women. God's love is not like human love; it's not primarily to do with what we feel. It's true that the love of God IS shed abroad in us by the Holy Ghost, but like Kathie in that meeting, we don't always feel it. But when you move out and ACT on it - you find it has been there all the time. God's love is first an act.

In Ezek 36:26-27 it says, "A new heart also will I give you, and a new spirit will I put within you: and I will take away the stony heart out of your flesh, and I will give you a heart of flesh. And I will put my spirit within you, and cause you to walk in my statutes, and ye shall keep my judgments, and do them."

32. Unbelief

A friend of mine was teaching a Bible Study in our home. The man had some bad allergies which really bothered him. I prayed for him, and as I did, I saw an angel leaning over him, encompassing him from behind. He was trying to bring healing to him. This angel had two enormous wings which came down behind him like a great train, like burnished gold. The man couldn't receive it because of his unbelief and wrong believing. It saddened me. "And he did not many mighty works there because of their unbelief" (Matt 13:58). A prayer group was praying for their church in Orlando. While they were praying for God to move in demonstration of His power and for healing and miracles, one lady had a vision of an angel. The angel was standing over the church, but his arms were bound with chains. The Lord spoke to them, "The angel of the Lord who has been sent to help you is bound because of unbelief." They realized that they were double minded; not sure if God wanted to really heal people. But you know the Bible says that when they brought the people to Jesus, He healed them ALL (Math 8:16). They repented over their unbelief and God began to move in healing in that church. Consequently, many people were healed and saved. In James, it says that a double-minded man cannot receive anything from God - you have to make a decision about what you believe and stand in faith, believing.

33. The Yardstick.

The Lord showed me a yardstick. I then saw the 1" mark and the Lord said to me, "See the yardstick? The 1" of obedience will bring a yardstick full of blessings. My blessings are not in proportion to your obedience." "Now unto him that is able to do exceeding abundantly above all that we ask or think, according to the power that worketh in us, Unto

Him be glory in the church by Christ Jesus throughout all ages, world without end. Amen" (Eph 3:20-21).

We can't earn anything from God. When we make the mistake of thinking that we can, we fail and come very short of receiving all that God has provided. We get to thinking that we have to "qualify". Jesus qualified us in the first place and you can't un-qualify from something you never qualified for in the first place. We are really weird sometimes!

34. *The Loons.*

I was praying with a group of ladies in my home when the Lord Jesus walked into the room. He was standing still and then huge wings on either side seemed to open. We all were encompassed under the wings. He spoke to us and said, "This is similar to the Loons which are here in New Hampshire; they carry their babies on their backs." Ps. 36:7 says, "How excellent is thy loving-kindness, O God! therefore the children of men put their trust under the shadow of thy wings."

Ps. 57:1 says, "Be merciful unto me, O God, be merciful unto me: for my soul trusteth in thee: yea, in the shadow of thy wings will I make my refuge..."

35. The Hem of His Garment.

I was in the bedroom watching a Christian TV program while waiting for my Monday ladies group to come. Jesus appeared before me in a white robe that I have seen Him in before. Overcome by His presence, I fell to my knees. I picked up the hem of His garment and kissed it. His eyes were like liquid love. He smiled gently at me and said, "Just the hem of my garments gives enough grace, mercy and forgiveness that you could ever need for your entire life." The sweetness of His presence stayed in the room. "Thou wilt shew me the path of life: in thy presence is fullness of joy; at thy right hand there are pleasures for evermore" (Ps. 16:11). On the hem of the priests garment were attached bells (the joyful sounds of the gospel and pomegranates - representing the sweet fragrant fruit of His presence. "Draw near to God and He will draw near to you." His grace and mercy is surely beyond our comprehension.

    I pray these words and visions will bless and encourage you in your relationship with your loving Lord.
                  -Thelma

This book is a publication of
Good News Ministries
220 Sleepy Creek Road
Macon, GA 31210
(478) 757-8071
Goodnews.netministries.org

Please call, write or visit the above website for further information on Good News Ministries and for information on their other published materials.

Formatting and editing for this book by Faith Dixon